PLANETARY WINDS

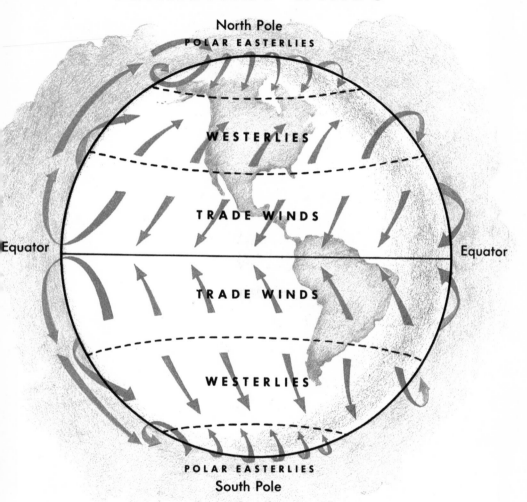

North Pole
POLAR EASTERLIES

WESTERLIES

TRADE WINDS

Equator — Equator

TRADE WINDS

WESTERLIES

POLAR EASTERLIES
South Pole

The earth turns this way ⟶

TORNADOES AND THEIR CLOUDS

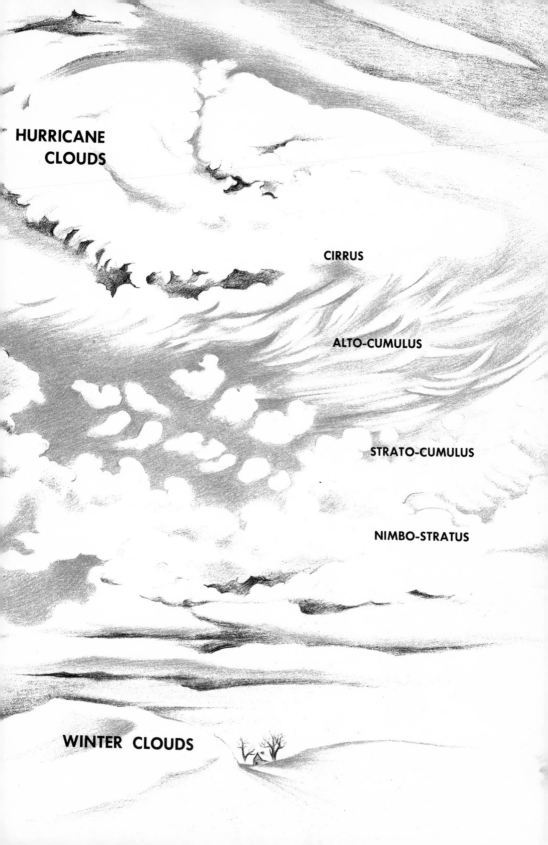

HURRICANE
CLOUDS

CIRRUS

ALTO-CUMULUS

STRATO-CUMULUS

NIMBO-STRATUS

WINTER CLOUDS

Hurricanes, Tornadoes, and Blizzards

HURRICANES
TORNADOES
and BLIZZARDS

by KATHRYN HITTE

illustrated by JEAN ZALLINGER

RANDOM HOUSE • NEW YORK

TO MY MOTHER AND FATHER

For helpful suggestions about the text and illustrations of this book, grateful acknowledgment is made to
ERNEST J. CHRISTIE
Meteorologist in Charge, United States Weather Bureau, New York City.

This title was originally catalogued by the Library of Congress as follows:

Hitte, Kathryn.
Hurricanes, tornadoes, and blizzards. Illustrated by Jean Zallinger. New York, Random House ₁1960₁

82 p. illus. 24 cm.

1. Storms—Juvenile literature.   I. Title.

PZ10.H54Hu   60—9423 ‡

Library of Congress   ₁61k5₁

Trade Ed.: ISBN:0-394-80115-6   Lib. Ed.: ISBN:0-394-90115-0

All rights reserved under International and Pan-American Copyright Conventions. Published in New York by Random House, Inc., and simultaneously in Toronto, Canada, by Random House of Canada, Limited.

Library of Congress Catalog Card Number: 60–9423

Manufactured in the United States of America

Contents

Hurricanes, Tornadoes, and Blizzards

1

Many storms

It is storming right now, somewhere in the world. Maybe it's only a thunderstorm, the kind of storm everyone knows. There are thousands of them every day.

But maybe a big, unusual storm is beginning—a storm of wild, strong winds that do terrible damage. Perhaps it is a storm that the papers will write about, that people will talk about and remember.

Perhaps it's a *blizzard*, that howling winter storm of wind and snow. Perhaps it's a *tornado*—the dreaded "twister," with the strongest wind in the world. Or perhaps it's the giant of all storms, and it is beginning like this:

The air is very warm and damp. There is hardly any wind. The waves of the sea are not at all like the usual steady-beating waves. Now they come slow and far between, in what is called a "long swell." Far in the distance, thin white clouds can be seen. They look like a scarf of some thin material floating very high in the sky.

Suddenly things are different. The weatherman can tell by his instruments that the air has changed. There is bad weather ahead. The high, thin clouds disappear, and dark clouds cover the sky. With a whoosh and a roar, the rain and wind arrive. Huge waves pound the shore. Almost at once the land is soaked and half-drowned. Houses are wrecked. Trees fall.

This is no everyday wind and rain. This is a *hurricane.*

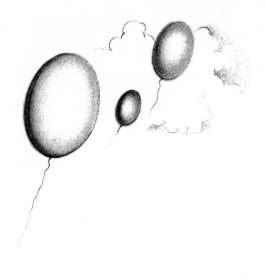

2

What is air?

To have a big storm, or to understand one, we have to start with air.

Air is everywhere around our earth. We cannot see it, or hold it with our hands, but we know that air is real, just the same. We know that we must breathe air to live. People have learned what air is like, and what it can do, and what happens to it sometimes.

You know some things that air can do.

It can fill balloons and bicycle tires. You know, too, that air has *temperature*. It can be hot or cold, warm or cool.

Air always has some water in it. Like the air itself, the water cannot be seen. In this form, it is called water vapor. Sometimes in hot weather, the air feels very damp. "It's so *humid!*" people say. This

In tires, air can support a truck that weighs tons.

means that the air has a great deal of water vapor in it. The amount of dampness in the air is called *humidity*.

Water vapor is important because it makes our rain and snow.

Air is always pushing against the earth. Air pushes against other air, too. This "push" is called *air pressure*. A spool and cardboard can prove that the air pushes. The picture on the next page shows how.

Air does not push with the same force all the time. When the air's push is strong, the pressure is called "high." "Low pressure" means a lighter push. In good weather the air pressure is usually high. In bad weather it is usually low.

Air is greedy. It is always trying to get more room for itself. If you empty a glass of water, air grabs the space at once, filling the glass. The same thing is happening all over the world, all the time. Air is always moving over the earth, trying to get more room.

This action of air makes many things

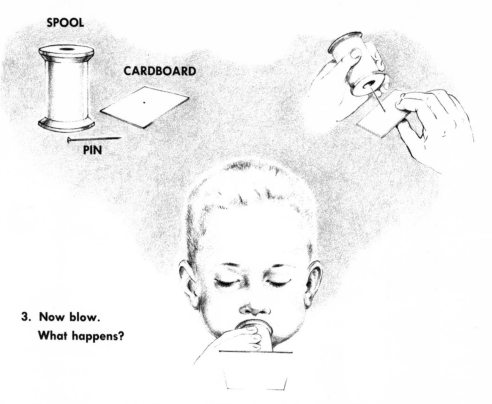

1. For this experiment with air pressure, you will need:

SPOOL

CARDBOARD

PIN

2. Put the pin through the cardboard, then into the hole.

3. Now blow. What happens?

happen to our weather. Temperature, humidity, and pressure make things happen, too. They work together to cause storms.

Weathermen study the air very carefully. They learn all they can about different kinds of air—warm and damp; cold and dry; and so on. They watch temperature, humidity, and pressure every day. They keep track of the movements of the air.

Then they can tell us what the weather will be like. They can warn us of storms ahead of time.

The picture shows some instruments that tell us about the weather.

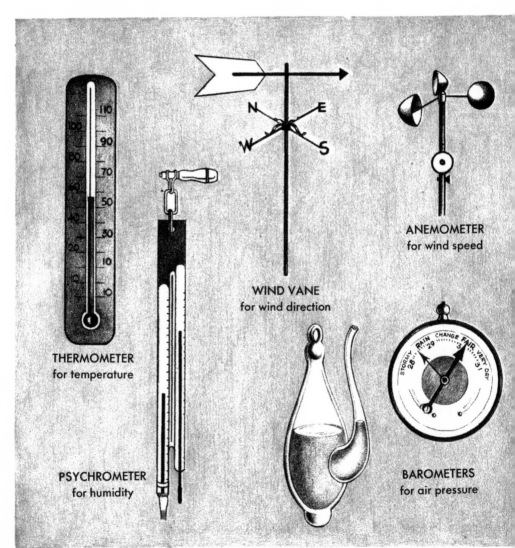

THERMOMETER
for temperature

PSYCHROMETER
for humidity

WIND VANE
for wind direction

ANEMOMETER
for wind speed

BAROMETERS
for air pressure

3

Busy winds

Wind is moving air.

When you fan yourself, you make the air move. This causes a little breeze that cools you. You feel wind when you run, or when you drive in an open car. Anything moving through air makes the air move, too.

But air can also start moving by itself. When the air becomes heated, winds begin. Warm air swells like a blown-up balloon.

This helps make it lighter than cool air. Because it is light, it rises. It floats upward.

As the warm air rises, it makes room for more air underneath. Then cooler air moves in to fill the space. The movement of the cooler air is what we call wind.

You can feel warm air rising. Hold your hand high above a pan of boiling water, higher than the cloud you see. You will feel heat on your hand. It comes from the air that has been warmed by the water. As soon as the water stops boiling, you will stop feeling warm air.

Everywhere, warm air and cool air act just the way they do over the stove. The sun heats the land and water of the earth. Then land and water heat the air above them. The warmed air rises, and cooler air pours in to take its place.

Air may move for other reasons, too. Sometimes different kinds of air meet. They push at each other, trying to get all the

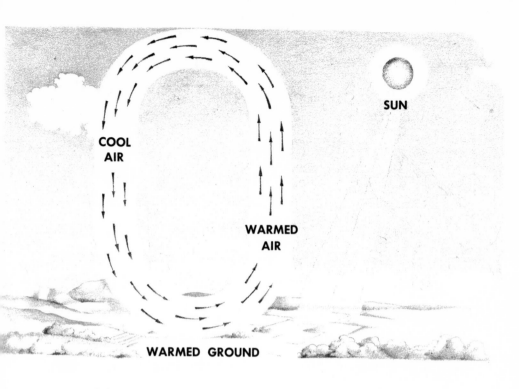

COOL
AIR

SUN

WARMED
AIR

WARMED GROUND

Warm air rises, leaving room for cool air to pour in.

room over that part of the earth. In the struggle, winds begin to blow.

When air moves fast enough for us to feel it, we may say, "That's a nice breeze." Or, "Goodness! What a wind!" If the wind blows wildly, at great speeds, we have a *windstorm.*

Wind is always blowing somewhere. Some winds we notice and some we do

13

not. Both kinds help to make our weather. Both have a lot to do with storms.

The winds we notice are the ones that blow close to the earth. They change often. And they do not blow all the time. Storm winds are this kind. So are the winds that push sailboats and turn windmills and cool us off after a hot day.

The winds we do *not* notice are the ones that blow very high above us. They are called *planetary winds*. They are always blowing around our planet, the earth. They blow over the whole earth, not just one part of it. They never stop. The planetary winds flow along somewhat like currents of water flowing in rivers and streams.

These air currents carry things with them, just as water currents can carry sticks and bottles along. The planetary wind currents help carry weather from place to place. They help carry cold air and warm air across the earth. When a storm grows up over one place, planetary winds often

PLANETARY WINDS

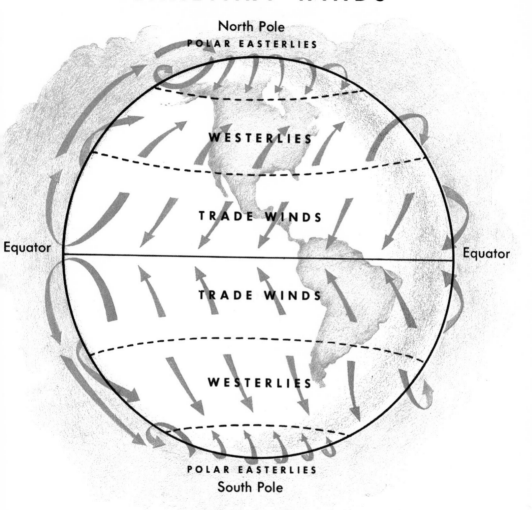

North Pole
POLAR EASTERLIES

WESTERLIES

TRADE WINDS

Equator

Equator

TRADE WINDS

WESTERLIES

POLAR EASTERLIES
South Pole

The earth turns this way

help carry it somewhere else. Blown by the great air currents, the same storm winds can hit many places, far apart.

Together, these two kinds of winds— storm winds and planetary winds—can make nasty weather for many people.

4

The giant hurricane

When explorers first came to Central America, they learned two Indian words: *Hurakan* and *hurican*. Hurakan was the name of a god some of the natives believed in. They thought this god sent all storms upon the earth. The word "hurican" meant evil spirit. If a person was mean and cruel, the natives might say a *hurican* was in him.

From those words we got our word *hurricane*—a good name for a cruel storm.

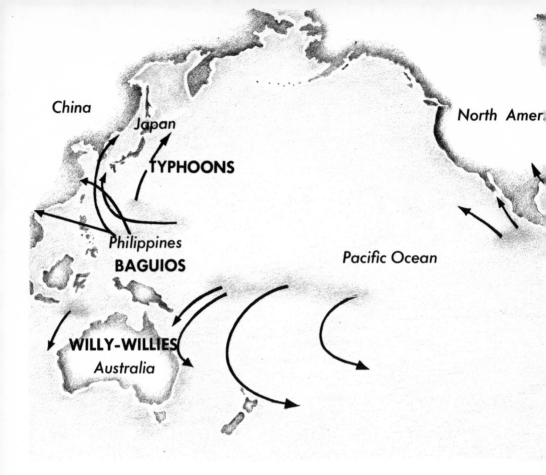

China
Japan
TYPHOONS
Philippines
BAGUIOS
WILLY-WILLIES
Australia
Pacific Ocean
North Amer.

In other parts of the world, the hurricane has other names. In some places it is called a *typhoon* or a *cyclone*. In other places it is called a *baguio* or a *willy-willy*. The map shows where the different names are used, and where the storms blow. You can see that the Far East suffers from typhoons, and India suffers from cyclones.

Not many hurricanes hit the United

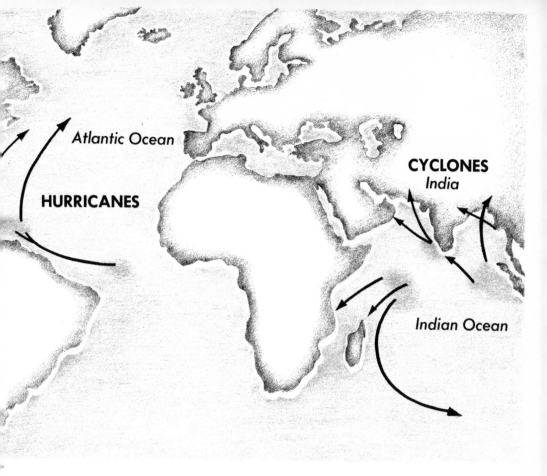

Atlantic Ocean

HURRICANES

CYCLONES
India

Indian Ocean

States. Some years there may be three or four, but other years only one. The average is about two a year. Others strike Mexico, Central America, and the nearby islands. But many more blow in the Atlantic Ocean and threaten danger to America. Weathermen are kept busy watching all of these.

Because there are so many hurricanes to watch, the United States Weather Bureau decided to name them. That way, they would be easier to keep track of.

So a list of girls' names is made up each year and given to the hurricanes in ABC order. Ann might be the first hurricane of the year, Betty the second one, and Cathy the third.

No matter what it is called, or where it blows, a full-grown hurricane is a big storm and a wild one. It generally blows for more than a week and travels for thousands of miles. When it tears over the land, it leaves death and great damage behind it. Most storms can strike only a very small region at one time. But when a hurricane hits one town, it hits many others at the same time. Its rain and wind are felt for hundreds of miles.

Put a penny in a saucer and compare the two things. If you imagine that the penny is the size of a town, then the saucer shows the size of a hurricane. This is why the hurricane is called a giant of a storm.

5

A hurricane is born

Where do hurricanes start?

Halfway between the North Pole and the South Pole lies the equator. The regions of the equator are the hottest parts of the earth. They always get a lot of sun, and their seas are very warm. Hurricanes are born in these warm oceans.

Most hurricanes start when the sun is almost straight overhead at the equator. Then the sun beats down fiercely. Many people, all around the earth, start to watch for signs of the storm.

Scientists know how a hurricane acts once it is started. But they do not know just *how* or *why* one begins. They can only try to figure out the reasons from certain things they do know. Some people have one idea, and some have another. Many say that this is what probably happens:

During the hottest months near the equator, the sea becomes very, very warm. It heats the air above it. The warmed air swells up and becomes lighter. It becomes so light that it rises swiftly, almost as if something were sucking it up. This upward movement is called an *updraft*.

From all around, and from miles away, cooler air pours in to take the place of the rising air. You know that the earth is always turning. As it turns, the winds of cool air turn, too. They curve in toward the updraft. They start to whirl, and they whirl faster and faster until they make a great whirlwind. Rain pours down.

The rain and the wind will both be worse before the hurricane is over. If the storm stays above the sea, it won't do much harm unless a ship gets too close. But if it blows over land, it can do great harm.

6

How the storm winds act

If you have ever seen a top moving across the floor while it is spinning, you have a good idea of how a hurricane acts. The whirling winds spin round and round, and at the same time they move along a curving path that covers many miles.

The hurricanes that come to North America have winds that whirl in one direction:

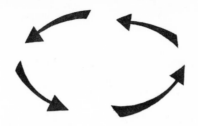

But their path goes in the other direction, like this:

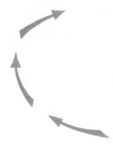

Here are the two motions put together:

If you trace these lines with your finger, starting at the big X, you will be able to "see" the action of the winds.

What makes the storm travel from the spot where it begins? It is carried along by planetary winds that are always blowing. All over the world, hurricanes move in great curves, for the same reason. The map on pages 18-19 shows the curving paths of hurricanes, cyclones, and typhoons.

Twist a strip of paper around a pencil, the way the drawing shows.

Now look at the pencil from above. The strip of paper shows the movement of the winds. Your pencil is the updraft of warm air. The winds whirl around that center of

Tremendous winds race around the calm eye of the hurricane.

rising air with an upward motion. They start at the bottom and spiral upward, just as your strip of paper does.

This spiral of winds stretches up to a height of eight miles or more—higher than the highest mountain.

The center of the whirling air is called the *eye* of the hurricane. When air moves straight up or down, we do not feel wind. So the eye of the hurricane is calm. All around the eye, for many miles, winds race at furious speeds. They reach 100 miles an hour, 150, 175, and even more.

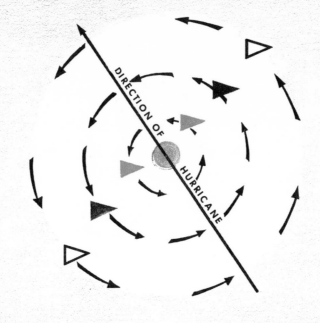

DIRECTION OF HURRICANE

The nearer they get to the eye, the faster they rush. No man could stand up against those winds. Yet the calm air of the eye may be only a short distance away.

The eye of the hurricane has fooled many persons when the storm passed over them. When they felt the still, peaceful air at the center they thought the hurricane was over. But in a little while winds were blowing fiercely again.

People standing in different sections of a hurricane might never agree on the direction of the wind. That is because the winds blow in a circle. The chart shows wind directions, too. You can tell the many directions by the many arrows. To see what a puzzle the wind direction can be, look at the man, the woman, and the ship on the chart. The man would be getting a wind from the north. The woman feels wind from the west. The ship feels it from the southeast.

In many ways, the hurricane is a very strange storm.

7

The storm grows and travels

A hurricane grows before it starts to travel, and it grows for a while as it travels. As long as it is over warm waters, it keeps on growing. There is more and more rain. The winds blow more and more fiercely and rush toward the eye from farther and farther away. So the storm stretches over more and more miles.

The drawing shows how the hurricane grows. It shows the different things that are going on in the air during the worst part of the storm.

Notice how the rain is made. That is the way all rain is made. As air rises, it cools, and its water vapor cools, too. This cooling changes the vapor into tiny droplets of water. They gather together in clouds. As more air cools, more and more vapor becomes water. At last the water in the clouds falls to earth as rain.

A hurricane seems to need very warm water in order to live. When it blows over

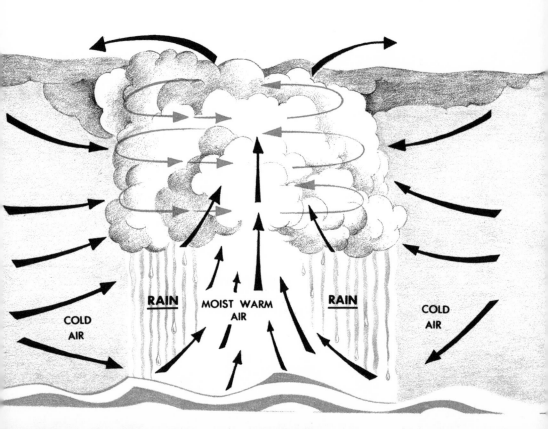

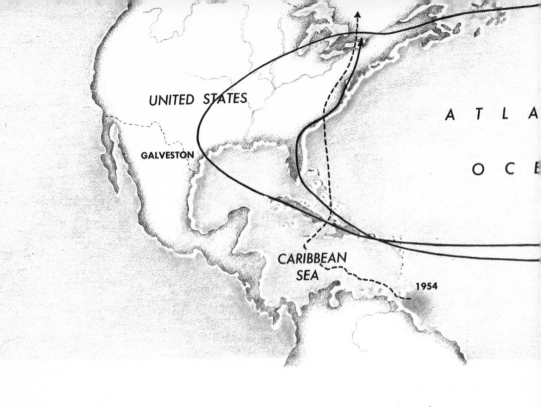

land, it stops growing. Soon it begins to lose its force. When it blows over cool waters, it slows down, too.

Most hurricanes live about nine days. Some of them die out over land, and some over water. Nearly all the ones that hit North America curve back into the ocean. The planetary winds carry them out over the North Atlantic, and there they die.

The map shows the travels of three hurricanes that visited North America in different years. Two of them began in a very

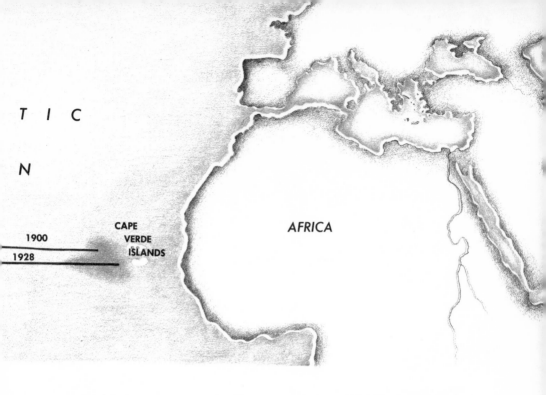

warm region near Africa. The other began
in the Caribbean Sea. You can find both
of those regions on the map. They are the
"homes" of North American hurricanes.

Many of these storms blow over American waters but never reach the land. Most
of those that do reach land stay only a day
or two before curving out to sea again.

But sometimes a hurricane does not fol-
low the usual path. Now and then one
stays longer over land. Then it makes big
news.

33

8
The power of wind and wave

A hurricane gives warning before it strikes. Air pressure falls swiftly from very high to very low. When the weatherman sees this change on his instruments, he looks for trouble. He knows that very low pressure means a big storm.

People who have seen many hurricanes can read warnings in the weather, the sea, and the sky. The still, humid air gives warning. The long, slow ocean waves give warning. So do the high white clouds before the dark rain clouds. People board up their windows. Many get ready to leave the seacoast. They hurry to protect themselves from the power of the storm.

As easily as you can blow out a candle, the hurricane's wind can blow buildings down. As easily as you can toss a ball, a hurricane wind can pick up chunks of stone the size of a car and carry them half a mile.

Full-grown trees are weak as weeds in such a wind. Up they come by the roots! Thick steel cables are twisted or snapped. Bridges break; tall towers fall. Ships at sea are battered by waves and tossed by the wind. Sometimes they are wrecked and sunk.

The picture on the opposite page shows something that happened during a hurricane in Puerto Rico. It shows how the wild wind drove a board right through a tree.

In a hurricane, there is something even more awful and more dangerous than the

wind. It is water. The greatest danger comes from the storm waves of the sea.

These are not like the ordinary waves that are always part of the sea. Storm waves are formed by the wind pushing the water. When the storm waves reach the shore, they become giants. They rise and rise. Then, like crumbling walls, they crash upon the land.

Storm waves have killed millions of people and animals, all over the world. They have washed away homes and flooded the land for miles. In India and Japan, whole towns have been drowned by waves higher than the houses.

North America has been luckier. Hurricane waves are not as huge as the waves of cyclones and typhoons. But Americans have seen some big ones. The worst one which flooded the town of Galveston, Texas, and killed 6,000 people. That was many years ago. Today, strong walls protect the town from the sea.

The hurricane's rain brings trouble, too.

No other hard rain is like it. Tons of water fall in a short time. Rain fills the rivers and soaks into the earth until rivers and earth can hold no more. Then great floods come. Soil may be washed away, and farmers' crops ruined.

Everyone is very glad when at last the weatherman reports: "The storm is dying out. Clearing tomorrow!"

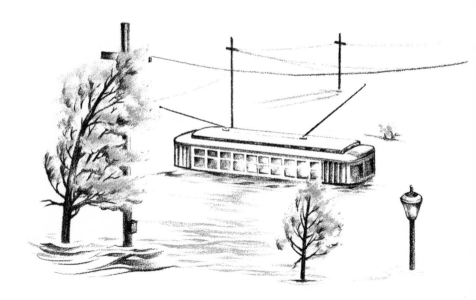

9

Tracking a hurricane

Before that report, "Clearing tomorrow," can be given, our weathermen have done a lot of work. They have tracked and studied the hurricane from the time it was born. The men who do this belong to the Hurricane Warning Service of the United States Weather Bureau.

In the picture on the next page, you will see some different ways of tracking American hurricanes. With all these helps, the

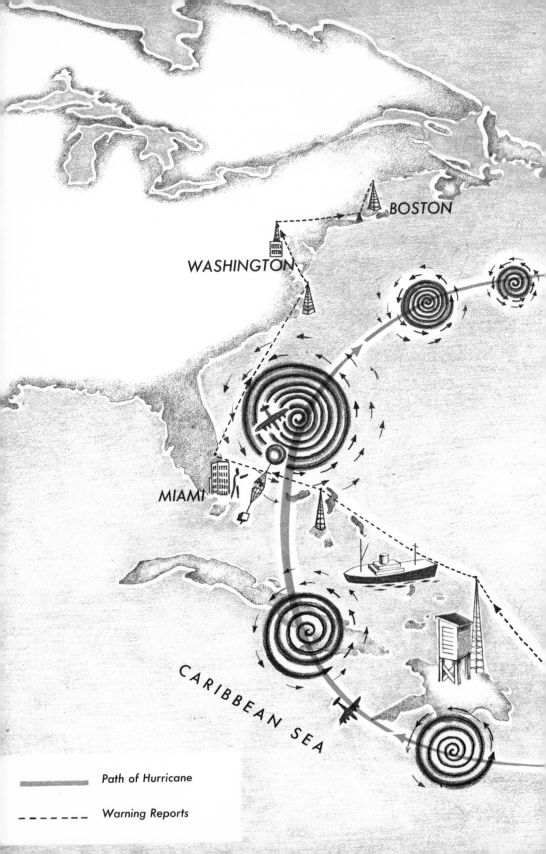

BOSTON

WASHINGTON

MIAMI

CARIBBEAN SEA

———————————— Path of Hurricane

– – – – – – – – Warning Reports

people of the Warning Service can tell at any time how big the storm is. They can tell where it is heading, how fast it is moving, and how strong its winds are.

The Hurricane Warning Service begins to keep watch as soon as a storm is reported near one of the homes of hurricanes. Even if the storm is a very mild, little one, it is important. It could grow into an angry giant. The storm tracked in this picture was one of those.

The first reports came from ships at sea. Later, the Warning Service sent out planes to fly right into the storm and see what kind it was. The planes went through the storm every six hours. The pilots found whirling clouds and heavy rain. They found a calm center, where the air was warm. The storm *was* a hurricane, and it was growing.

Soon warnings went out to the islands that lay in the hurricane's path. Ships at sea were warned, too. Later, towns along the east coast of the United States were warned. People had time to find safety.

The picture shows the three stations of the Hurricane Warning Service. The station in Miami does the most work every year, because it tracks all the hurricanes that head toward America. Even if they never arrive, this station is kept busy. If they do threaten, the stations in Washington and Boston may go to work, too.

Now weather satellites in orbit above the earth spot new storms and send back signals reporting on them. Weathermen who receive the signals can give quicker warnings than ever before.

Only a few years ago, there was no special Warning Service. The great storms often took people by surprise and caused many deaths. Hurricanes still can play tricks on us, but they cannot surprise us completely any more.

There is another storm that is not so easy to track—a storm even more powerful than the hurricane. That is the *tornado*.

10
Tornado coming!

Once in Nebraska a group of students had a great adventure. Not many people have done what they did. They looked up into the center of the most powerful storm on earth. They saw what went on inside a tornado.

The students were in a park on a warm spring day. The air was the kind of air that people call "heavy"—very still and breathless. In the sky was a great, dark, puffy thundercloud. The cloud and some of the sky were an odd, ugly color—a sort of green.

And hanging from the thundercloud was a long narrow cloud, like a finger from the sky.

"Tornado!" someone shouted.

Before the young people could run to find shelter, the finger of cloud whirled toward them. For a moment it hung right over their heads. They looked up and saw into it.

It was a huge hollow thing, rather like a tube. It was very black inside, except that flashes of sharpest lightning tore through it every second. Whirling clouds showed in the flashes of light. From the hollow "tube" came a roaring and a hissing and a high screaming.

"Like millions of bees," one of the students said later. "Like ten thousand freight trains," others said.

The cloud whirled away, and the students were safe. A few miles off, the tornado

reached for the ground. It wrecked what-
ever it touched.

That long narrow cloud is made of
whirling winds—winds so fierce that no
one knows just how strong they are. They
do no harm while the cloud hangs in the
air. But when it touches the earth—*look
out!*

11
Strongest wind in the world

Sometimes a huge amount of cold air, blowing over the earth, meets a lot of warm air. The two air masses crash into each other. The cold air tries to squeeze under the warm air and at the same time push it all out of the way.

When the air masses in this struggle are very different from each other, their battle is especially fierce. That is what happens with the air masses when a tornado begins.

Weathermen know only one other thing about the making of a tornado. Before the whirling, narrow cloud can grow, cold air somehow gets blown *above* warm air. The warm air is trapped. Its winds struggle fiercely to get out of the trap. The winds of the cold air struggle to get *under* the warm air. A huge black cloud forms above the earth where the battle is going on. In

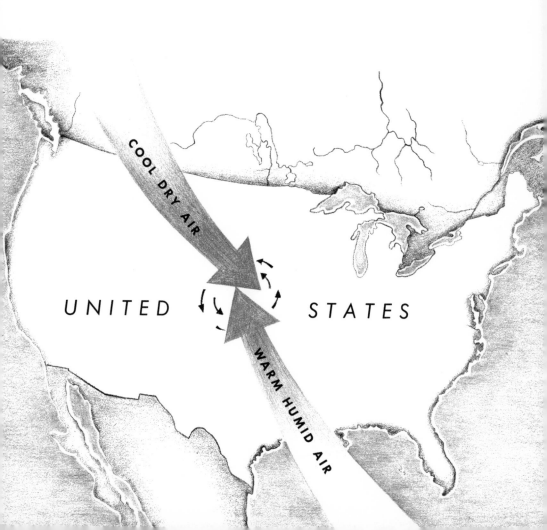

COOL DRY AIR

UNITED STATES

WARM HUMID AIR

the cloud there is a great stirring and churning and boiling.

During the struggle, two things happen. No one quite knows how. A whirlwind starts, and air rushes upward in the middle of the whirlwind. The air becomes filled with electricity. Then lightning is seen and thunder heard. The updraft grows, and the whirlwind grows.

And down from the big thundercloud comes the whirling wind, in a strange cloud of its own.

The tornado's wind blows with a force much greater than that of any hurricane. It is the strongest wind we know, and it makes the most violent storm.

Men have tried to measure the force of the tornado wind. Their instruments recorded a speed of 300 miles an hour—and then broke. Some scientists think that the winds blow at 500 or 600 miles an hour. They think some big tornadoes may have winds of 800 miles an hour. That is faster than a jet plane breaking the sound barrier.

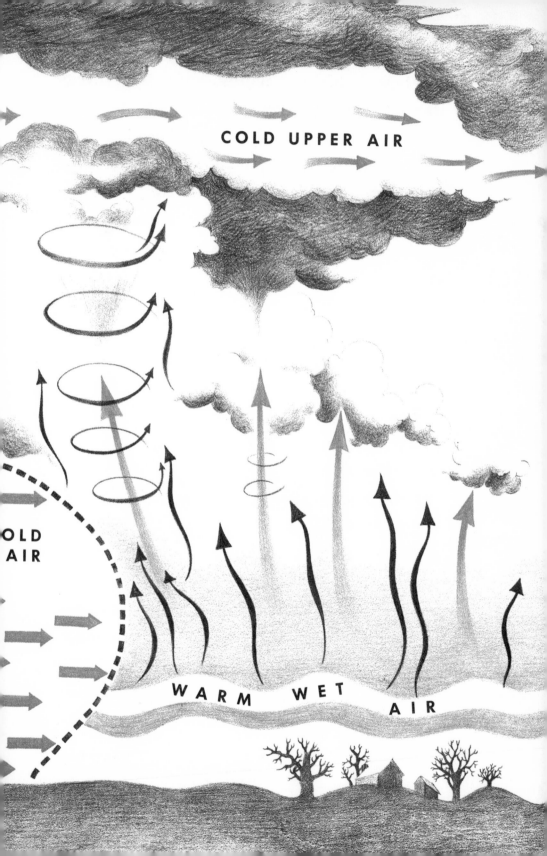

These whirling winds, and the things they do, have given the tornado a nickname: "twister." One twist—and a car goes swirling through the air. Another—and a great bridge is torn apart. "Twister" is a good nickname for such a storm.

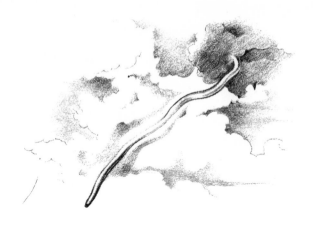

12
Strange tricks

The finger of cloud coming down to earth is the special sign of a tornado. Weathermen call this cloud the *vortex*. Most people call it the *funnel*.

The vortex cloud may hang straight down, hardly seeming to move. It may wiggle gently in the air, or lash about like a cracking whip. Wherever it touches the ground, terrible wreckage follows. Sometimes it wipes out everything in its path.

The whirling winds make up the funnel. The great updraft is inside it. These are what give the tornado its great power, and they probably cause the hideous noise that is always heard.

Have you ever whirled a ball on a string swiftly around your head? The ball does not flop loosely. It strains at the end of the tightly stretched string. That is the way the winds of the tornado funnel act. They move so fast that they stay along the "walls" of the funnel. So the center of the funnel is almost without air.

A place without air is a *vacuum*. The tornado's vortex is a *partial vacuum*—that is, partly a vacuum. You know what a vacuum cleaner does to everything it touches. That is the way the partial vacuum of the tornado acts. It sucks up roofs, houses, and cars. It sucks up animals and fences from fields, and water out of wells. It sucks up plenty of dirt from the ground, too. All this helps to make the tornado cloud black and ugly.

Objects picked up by the funnel may be set down unharmed at another place, a few yards away—or miles away. Sometimes they are twisted and broken, or only a few pieces are found. But sometimes they are never found at all.

Since the center of the funnel is almost

without air, it has very little air pressure. This extremely low pressure sometimes makes buildings explode. When the funnel passes directly over a building, the air pressure *in* the building suddenly becomes much greater than the pressure around it outdoors. So the building bursts like a balloon.

That is a strange thing, but not so strange as some of the tricks tornadoes have played. A man was once blown into the air and wrapped up in a wire fence. He lived to be unwrapped and tell the story! Tornadoes have set heavy iron weights down on glass without breaking the glass. They have stripped all the feathers from chickens, and left the chickens alive.

A tornado's wind can blow a straw of wheat deep into wood like a knife, without bending the straw. Once a burning lamp was carried some distance by the great whirlwind. An ordinary puff of wind would blow out such a lamp—but this lamp was still burning when it was found.

13
Tornado playground

If you live in any of the Great Plains states, you live in "Tornado Playground." You have a good chance of seeing a twister sometime in your life.

Over and over, tornadoes have struck this region.

Many parts of the world have these storms, but the most and the worst come to the United States. Hundreds of tornadoes strike somewhere in the United States every

A storm cellar

year. About half of them hit the "playground" of the Middle West.

The people of these states sometimes have special places in which to hide. They have made caves, or cellars, underground. At the first sign of the twister, people can dash for the nearest storm cellar. In these cellars, the whirling funnel cannot reach them.

Why should the Middle West be a special target for tornadoes? Because that same region is one of the big "battlegrounds" of the air. It is the meeting place of two very different air currents. Air from the north and air from the Gulf of Mexico meet over the Great Plains. The two air masses are very different from each other. So they have fierce battles.

From the power of the tornado, weathermen have decided that these battles are probably the fiercest that ever go on above the earth.

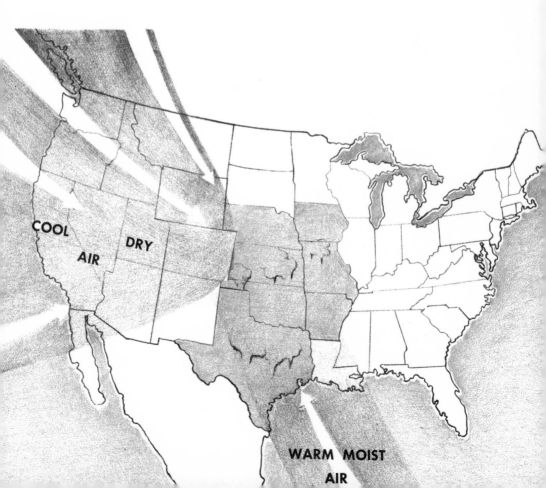

COOL AIR

DRY

WARM MOIST AIR

14

Just a speck on the map

Compared to a hurricane, the tornado is only a speck on the map.

On the next page, the second map shows the state of Kansas hit by a tornado. The first map shows what would happen if a hurricane ever came directly over Kansas.

A tornado is hardly ever more than 350 yards wide. You could step off that distance in 350 long steps. Many twisters are even narrower, sometimes only as wide as a road.

The storm is little in other ways, too. It nearly always makes a quick visit and a short journey. It does not stay more than half a minute in any one spot. It moves along its narrow path for only fifteen or twenty miles. Often it "skips" on the path. The funnel lifts and falls, lifts and falls. So some ground along the path is untouched.

Then, in twenty minutes or half an hour, the storm is over. The funnel has disap-

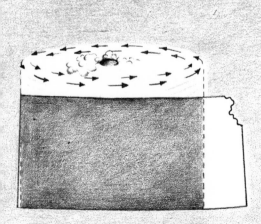

HURRICANE OVER KANSAS

TORNADO OVER KANSAS

peared. Where did it go? Back into the big thundercloud. Why is the storm over so quickly? Nobody knows. It simply wears itself out.

The tornado's little size and short life are the only good things about it. They make its great power seem even more amazing. If twisters lasted as long as hurricanes—well, that is not a pleasant thing to think about.

Just as other storms do, tornadoes travel with the planetary winds. The air currents that blow over most of the United States are called the westerly winds. You can find them in the drawing on page 15. These winds blow from the west toward the northeast. So the tornado's path is usually northeast.

Sometimes a twister goes in another direction. Sometimes a storm lasts for hours and travels much farther than most tornadoes. The longest twister ever reported went 293 miles without a skip.

The worst tornado America has ever

had was a very strange one. No one saw a funnel. Along a path more than 200 miles long, the storm was seen only as a mass of foggy blackness rolling close to the earth.

This storm was the "Great Tri-State Tornado" of 1925. It roared across Missouri, Illinois, and Indiana, killing 689 people and injuring almost 1,500 others. It caused more deaths and damage than any other twister in our history.

The tornado that does the least damage is a tornado over the sea. Then it is called a *waterspout*. It sucks a long column of water from the ocean into the sky, and the fishes get a free ride in the air.

15
A problem for
the weatherman

Tornadoes are the weatherman's "problem storm." They give little warning of their coming. So they are very hard to forecast. Besides, the struggling air masses always cover many miles of the earth. So the weatherman cannot tell exactly where one "little" twister will strike.

Even when he knows a funnel has been seen, he cannot warn many people. The twister is gone too quickly. It cannot be

followed and studied before it does damage, as the hurricane can.

What does the weatherman do, then? He watches for weather that reminds him of tornado weather. He watches all his instruments for signs of great struggles in the air. He gets reports from a pilot who flies for the Weather Bureau, all around "Tornado Playground." The pilot searches for signs of tiny funnels in the clouds.

Sometimes the weatherman can only

warn people of bad weather and storms in general. But other times he feels surer, and can say, "Tornadoes are very likely over the state today."

Then the people in the region keep their own watch for the odd-colored sky. They look out for the ugly cloud and the funnel.

The Weather Bureau is working hard to learn more about tornadoes, and to find better ways of warning. Army, Navy, and Air Force weathermen are working with the United States Weather Bureau, and so are other scientists.

They are all trying out some new inventions that may be able to spot a tornado before men can do it. Rockets and satellites high in the air take pictures of the storms from above. Weathermen hope the pictures will teach them more about how tornadoes form and act.

If the studies and experiments are successful, men may someday be able to forecast a tornado. The twister will still blow over our land, but lives will be saved.

16

Winter windstorm

The snows of winter fall upon many lands of the earth. It is then that another kind of fierce windstorm is born. *Blizzards* blow over many countries both north and south of the equator.

The drawing on the next page shows the regions that are called the "home" of blizzards. They are the regions around the North Pole and the South Pole. Cold air blows from those regions across much of

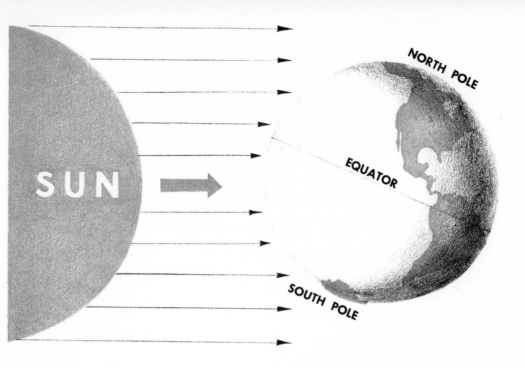

North America gets less heat and light in winter.

the earth. During the winter seasons this *polar air* is very, very cold. It has had no sunshine for months.

When polar air blows over a land in the wintertime, snowstorms often come with it. The storms begin when a mass of polar air crashes into a mass of warm air full of water vapor. The cold air and the warm air struggle for all the space they can get, and winds begin.

The polar air usually wins this battle, because extremely cold air is very heavy.

It is able to push under the warm air and lift it. It takes up all the room directly above the earth. The warm air is pushed high, high up. There, far above the earth, the temperature is always very cold. It is so cold that the water vapor in the air freezes and becomes snow. Then snow clouds form—clouds filled with millions of snowflakes, just as rain clouds are filled with raindrops. Soon the snowflakes are falling to earth.

When fierce winds and great cold come along with the snow, the storm is a blizzard. Sometimes, if there is little water vapor in the air, wind and cold make a blizzard without a snowfall. The wind picks up "old" snow from the ground, and blows it so hard it seems to come from the sky.

The wind of a blizzard may be as strong as a hurricane wind. It makes the cold more dreadful and the snow more dangerous than they would be by themselves. People who live in wintry lands hate the blizzard's bitter wind.

17
The great blizzard

The worst blizzard ever known in the United States came in 1949.

It was really made up of six great blizzards. But they came one right after another. So people thought of them as one big storm.

The wind and snow and dreadful cold lasted for seven weeks. Ten Western and Middle Western states were hit hard. Day after day the winds blew—week after week.

Most of the time they blew with hurricane force—80 miles an hour, or more. Temperatures went down and down, to far below zero. Sometimes the snow stopped falling for a few days. But then the wild winds would blow the ground snow into higher and higher drifts.

Thousands of travelers were stalled in cars and in trains. Many small towns were cut off from the world by snow as high as the houses.

People died trying to walk only a short way in the storm. And on the ranchlands, about a million sheep and cattle died. They froze to death, or were buried by snow drifts. Many starved when the snow covered their pastureland.

Whenever the wind died down a little, crews of brave men got busy. They worked hard trying to keep roads clear and to bring help to trapped people and animals. Sometimes the storm would rise again while the men were working, and then the job seemed almost hopeless.

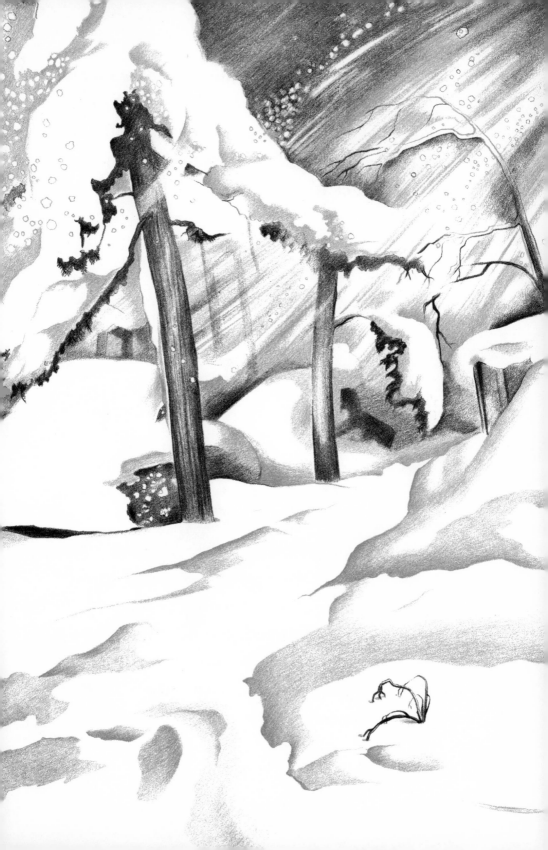

But at last the long stormy weeks ended. People were able to "dig out" and stay out. They have been talking about the "Big Snowstorm" ever since. They will never forget it.

18
A well-behaved storm

There are not many winter storms like that one, even in cold countries. But there are hundreds of smaller blizzards every year. In some parts of the world, blizzards may come from early September until April. The world's weathermen are kept busy forecasting and tracking these storms.

Compared to hurricanes and tornadoes, blizzards are well-behaved storms. They don't give the weatherman much trouble.

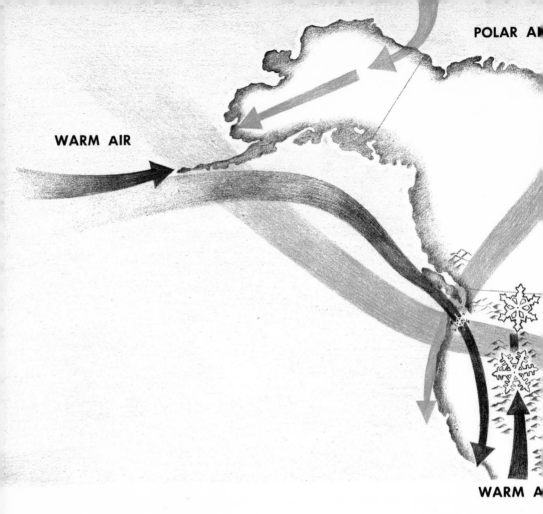

POLAR AI

WARM AIR

WARM A

Most blizzards give plenty of warning before they arrive. They start when they are expected to start, and go where they are expected to go.

The map shows some things that weathermen know about winter air over North America. It shows the paths of the winter air masses which blow over most of the

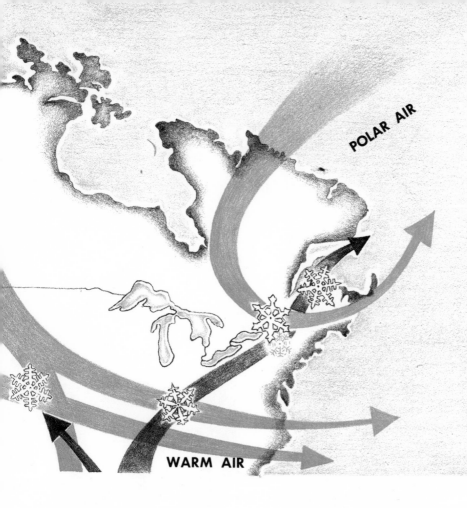

POLAR AIR

WARM AIR

United States. The snowflakes mark the regions where blizzards most often begin.

Blizzards are great travelers. They usually move with the same winds that carry tornadoes—the westerly winds. So if a storm has already begun in the west, weathermen can warn people farther east. The warnings may keep going out for days, for a blizzard can cross the country without dying down. It often has as long a life as a hurricane. It will make farms and cities over thousands of miles shiver in its cold north wind, and plow through its snow.

19
Big blow

Year in and year out, the storm winds blow. If you live almost anywhere in the United States, you are likely to see a "big blow" sometime in your life. Of all the states, only Hawaii has no hurricanes, no tornadoes, and no blizzards. Most parts of the world know at least one kind of big storm.

Long, long ago, people thought there was wicked magic in storms. Even today many people believe that way. They do not know what makes a storm. So they are more afraid than they need to be. *You* are one of the lucky people, because you know the truth. If a storm strikes, you will take shelter. But you will not be afraid of magic. You know that storms are a part of nature. They are as old as the earth itself. You know that scientists are working all the time to learn more about storms, so that we can protect ourselves better.

Somewhere in the world, it is storming right now—just as it was when you began this book. How about the weather where you are?

Listen. Was that thunder? Look at the sky. Do you see any signs of a storm?

Index

About the author of this book

Kathryn Hitte was born in Illinois, where she became familiar with tornadoes and blizzards. In New York City, where she and her husband now live, she has experienced the effects of hurricanes.

Miss Hitte graduated from Illinois College. As a young people's librarian for several years, she learned much about the reading tastes of boys and girls. For the past ten years, she has been writing fiction and non-fiction for young readers, including four previous books.

About the illustrator of this book

Jean Zallinger's scientific drawings have appeared in *Life, Natural History,* and other magazines. Among the books she has illustrated are *In the Days of the Dinosaurs* (an Easy-to-Read Book) and *All About Monkeys.*

Mrs. Zallinger studied at the Massachusetts School of Art and received a bachelor's degree from the Yale School of Fine Arts. With her husband, three children, and assorted household pets, she lives near New Haven, Connecticut.

THE RANDOM HOUSE GATEWAY SCIENCE LIBRARY

Physical Science and Mathematics

Your Wonderful World of Science	by Mae and Ira Freeman
Simple Machines and How They Work	by Elizabeth N. Sharp
The Story of the Atom	by Mae and Ira Freeman
The Story of Electricity	by Mae and Ira Freeman
The Story of Chemistry	by Mae and Ira Freeman
The Story of Numbers	by Patricia Lauber

Space and Astronomy

The Sun, the Moon, and the Stars	by Mae and Ira Freeman
The Earth in Space	by John and Cathleen Polgreen
The World of Rockets	by Alexander L. Crosby
Satellites in Outer Space	by Isaac Asimov

Earth and Weather

Rocks All Around Us	by Anne Terry White
In the Days of the Dinosaurs	by Roy Chapman Andrews
Danger! Icebergs Ahead!	by Lynn and Gray Poole
Hurricanes, Tornadoes, and Blizzards	by Kathryn Hitte

Life Science

Your Body and How It Works	by Patricia Lauber
Mammals and How They Live	by Robert M. McClung
The Friendly Dolphins	by Patricia Lauber
The Surprising Kangaroos	by Patricia Lauber

TORNADOES AND THEIR CLOUDS

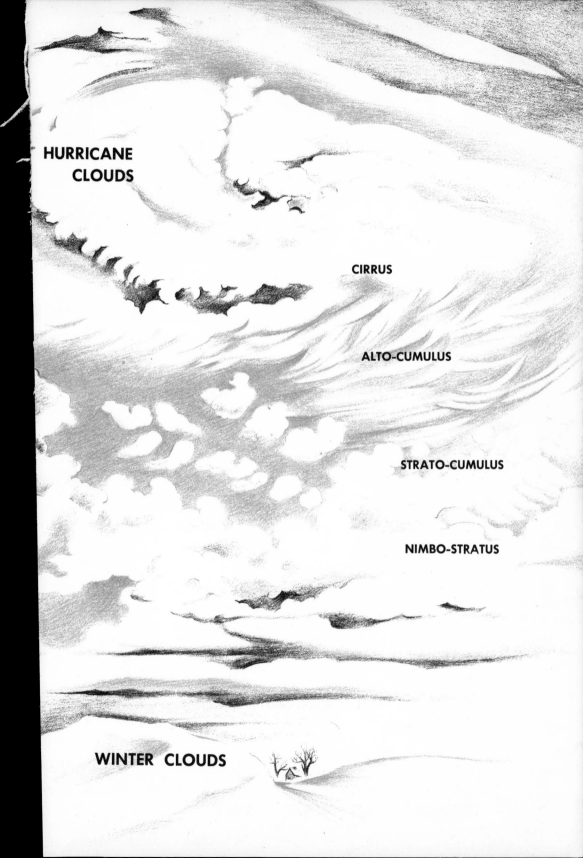

HURRICANE
CLOUDS

CIRRUS

ALTO-CUMULUS

STRATO-CUMULUS

NIMBO-STRATUS

WINTER CLOUDS

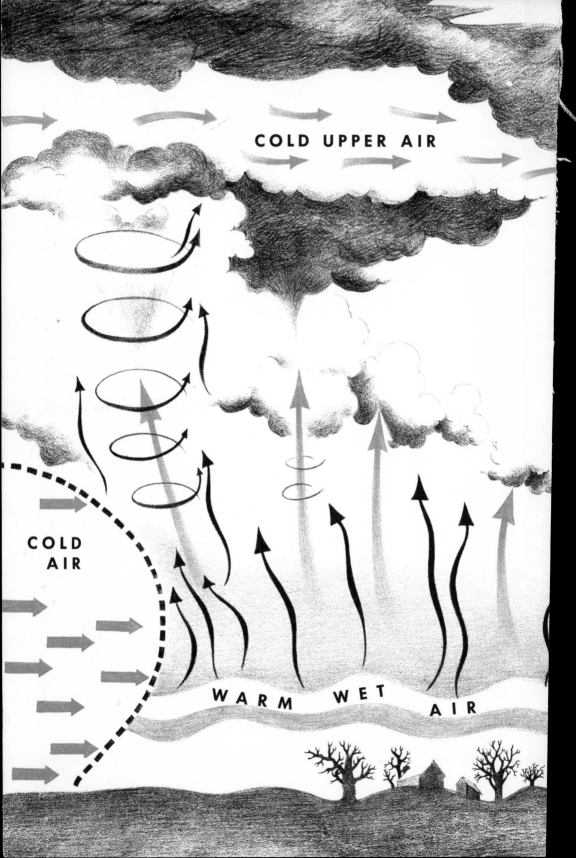

COLD UPPER AIR

COLD
AIR

WARM WET AIR